Jamie's Journey
"Travels with My Dad"

by Jamie Goodman

Foreward by Dr. Rick Goodman
author of *Living a Championship Life*
"A Game Plan for Success"

ISBN: 1492860301
ISBN 13: 9781492860303
Library of Congress Control Number: 2013919746
CreateSpace Independent Publishing Platform
North Charleston, South Carolina

DEDICATION

I would like to dedicate this book to my best friend and brother, Alex; my mom, Laurie, for always being there for me as both a friend and a mother; and my father for taking me on this incredible journey and teaching me life lessons that I could never have learned in a classroom. Lastly, I would like to dedicate this book to Jackie Klein Goodman; your strength and willingness to fight for those eight years was to be admired and commended. You instilled within me strength I never knew I had, and I cannot thank you enough for being a part of my life. I know wherever you are, you are looking down on us, and I hope you're proud. This book's for you!

Jackie and me celebrating Hanukkah with the Miami Heat

CONTENTS

ACKNOWLEDGMENTS

It is important that I recognize certain people without whose dedication and help this book would have not been possible. First I would like to thank Shirley Dingcong, my dad's executive assistant, who spent weeks typing up my journal entries. I would also like to thank Bruce Turkel for his marketing and branding ideas that helped me to formulate Jamie's Gems. I would also like to thank Will and Phoebe Ezell for their artistic insight and communication expertise and Susanne Jacoby-Hale for her editing expertise. Lastly I would like to thank my dad, Rick. If not for his belief in my writing skills and me, this book would not have been possible.

FOREWARD

By Dr. Rick Goodman

When I first spoke to Jamie about going to Europe for two weeks she was excited! Then I got the idea that we were already in Europe; how far away could Israel possibly be? Now the trip has turned into a twenty-four-day adventure covering three continents and five countries. As I made the itinerary I had the feeling that plans and teenagers don't always work the way you want them to. I also thought this would be a great opportunity for the two of us to write a book together. As you'll soon see, I have Jamie's personal journals, which contain "Gems" that she shares and that will help parents and children alike to better understand each other. It is my hope that the "Revelations" I share about our journey together stimulate parents to take the opportunity of a lifetime in this age of technology to really get to know their children.

As I was thinking about the first chapter of the book all that kept popping into my head was the following:

"Manage your expectations. Make your itinerary and be prepared to break it!"

Having this thought, I was truly unprepared for its effects before the trip even started. I made all of my plans, including a plane flight that would put me in St. Louis a day before we left for our journey. That way I would feel much more comfortable knowing that Jamie was prepared, and she would have everything she needed for our trip! The only problem was I did not discuss this with my daughter in advance. So two days before I was about to leave on the first leg of my trip, Jamie said to me, "Dad, no offense, but I want to hang out with my friends the night before I leave with you. After all, we're going away for three weeks alone together. Isn't that enough?"

Now I went into panic mode, rearranging my plans, and we had not even left! I thought I might have to change my itinerary, but not this fast. So reluctantly I booked my flight, losing all the money on the original trip, and altered my plans. Dealing with a teenager can be unpredictable at best when making arrangements! What was I thinking that everything would go smoothly without a hitch?

Rick's Revelation:

- *The key lesson is to go with the flow. If you're uptight about schedules get over it because magical things happen when you let the universe unfold as it should!*

JAMIE'S POINT OF VIEW

July 14, 2012

Here we go. I'm now at the age of sixteen, almost seventeen and I am about to embark on the hardest obstacle I have ever faced. I am about to travel on a twenty-four-day trip with my father. During this time we will be traveling to London, Paris, Florence, Rome, and the end, Israel. He has asked me to keep a journal throughout the trip, as a way to record not only my feelings about the beautiful sites we will be seeing, but also my emotions toward him. Now at this time you all should know something about my dad, which is that he is a HUGE New Yorker. He's the kind of guy who always yells, "YO" all the way across a restaurant to get our waiter's attention. Rick (my dad) has a voice that makes it seem like he is always yelling, even if he's not. But the number-one thing you should know about my dad is that he always has to be right, and he always has to have the last word. Well, as most say, the apple doesn't fall far from the tree, because with me, I never allow him that satisfaction.

In T-minus four days I will be embarking on this journey; it will be survival of the fittest, a last-man-standing kind of thing. Though we may be in different countries, the rules will apply, and only time will tell how long we will survive.

Jamie Goodman

CHAPTER 1

No Turning Back

Today was the day, and there was no turning back. It was the day I would finally start my worldwide journey with my dad. But before we entered the beautiful city of London we had to make a pit stop in Chicago; this is where the real adventure began.

While awaiting our three-hour layover in Chicago, my dad and I met a lady named Deloris Love. Now I must tell you another thing you should know about my dad: every time someone greets him and asks how he is doing today, he responds by saying, "I woke up!" There are many different reactions from people when he says this; some laugh, and some just smile while secretly giving that "I don't know how to respond" face, and then there are people like Deloris. Her eyes lit up as she extended her hand to shake my father's hand. "Can I shake your hand, Sir?" she asked with a smile that consumed her face. "Of course you can," my father said. From that moment it felt like we had been standing there talking forever.

My dad has that gift with people; he is able to connect with strangers, and by the end of his conversation with them he knows practically their whole life story. Well, after meeting Deloris, we continued what was left of our layover by sitting in the Admiral's Club. This is where I heard the most beautiful English accents; this is where we met Jim and Fran.

Jim and Fran were from Devon, England. Jim was a former British Air Force colonel. And he had been married to Fran for fifty-six years. They first caught our attention when I overheard Jim say they butchered the salmon in the airport lounge. Upon boarding the plane we noticed that they were sitting right behind us, and they were excited to share with us the wisdom of a lifetime of travel. My dad and I engaged in conversation with them on our British Airways flight to London. As I was captivated by their beautiful

British accents, I hung on to every word they spoke. The four of us engaged in conversation that seemed to never stop; we must have lost track of time because before I knew it, we had four hours and thirty minutes before we would be landing. I quickly realized it would be best to go to sleep, so I strapped my seatbelt on over my covers and fell asleep, unaware of the day I would have ahead of me.

Dad & me in our First Class pajamas courtesy of British Airways.

Rick's Revelations:

- *If you want to remain as stress-free as possible arrive an hour before you normally would! By doing this, Murphy's Law will be kept at bay. If you're traveling overseas come prepared to connect and be aware of the one-eyed monster called jetlag! This could be a parent's worst nightmare, because not only are you tired, but your child will be too, no matter what he or she says.*

- *If you want to be a Clark Griswold and hit every tour on the first day your trip will most definitely get off on the wrong foot, and you will run into your first challenge!*

- *Get comfortable quick! The flight overseas is not a fashion show to impress but an opportunity to get prepared for your first day. Connect, eat, and go to sleep!*

CHAPTER 2

Jet Lagged

There is a stage of being tired, or asleep, but then there is a stage of being so exhausted that you hallucinate what is going on, and you don't even know where you are. This feeling is what we call jet lag. I like to think it is something like a hangover (not that I would know). The fatigue one feels when experiencing jet lag is unimaginable until experiencing it head-on. When we stepped off the plane that day, I felt the jet lag and the exhaustion that I had only heard and read about.

Days before my father and I began our trip, he would tell me, "Jamie, once we get onto the flight to London we need to go to sleep as soon as possible so that we don't experience so much jetlag on the first day." Though I believed him, I thought, "What are you talking about? Jet lag couldn't be that bad, could it?" As soon as I awoke we landed in London; when we got off the plane we headed to the hotel to drop off the luggage. Since we had landed around 10:00 a.m., we wanted to make sure not to waste the day, and we headed to the famous Tower Bridge. I did not know it yet, but within an hour our jet lag would kick back in, and the real adventure would begin.

Crossing the Tower Bridge we went to the Tower of London Museum. Though seeing the Crown Jewels was fascinating, I shortly found myself dozing off and doing these awkward head bobs I always do on planes when I fall asleep. As we followed a tour guide, I got dizzy and became unaware of my surroundings. When I looked over to my dad he was stumbling around and experiencing the same side effects. But our last side effect was the most extreme. We hallucinated. At that time if someone had told me I was still in St. Louis I would have believed him. One could possibly describe this experience as being ruffled; everything was blurry, and I couldn't stay awake, and for once, coffee could not cure me, or should I say us! We both finally agreed to go back to the hotel, and in seconds we passed out on the beds, with no sign of waking up anytime soon. When we finally woke up, we showered, got dressed, and went for a quick bite of dinner. Once again, we arrived back at the hotel, and we passed out in minutes.

Jet lagged at the Tower Bridge.

Jamie's Gem:

- Whenever traveling abroad, always sleep on the plane ride, and don't plan on making any plans on the first day you arrive. If you follow this rule, you will most likely survive your first day with your dad or whomever you may be adventuring with.

CHAPTER 3

Connecting at the Palace

We are all somehow tied together; whether it's a blood relation, or a friend of a friend, we are all connected. This belief of mine was proven multiple times, beginning with our second day in London. While in London, one thing a tourist should not miss out on is the changing of the guards at Buckingham Palace. Though I will never understand the fascination with this ten-minute event that takes forty-five minutes to wait for, my dad and I went anyway.

As we stood waiting for the ceremony to begin, we wanted to move up closer to get a good picture. Since the place was crowded, my dad asked a lady standing against the railing if I could squeeze in next to her. We soon engaged in conversation with this woman, her husband, and daughter, and we found out that they were from Durango, Colorado. Shortly after, we learned that the wife had worked for a rock-climbing business, one just like our cousin Joseph used to work for. My dad suddenly reached for his iPhone and went on Facebook and pulled up a picture of our cousins. Well, to make a long story short, our cousin Joseph and Michelle were good friends with this family and Joseph used to work for the woman. The world just keeps getting smaller!

After we got out of the chaos at Buckingham Palace, we headed over to the British Museum, where we saw the Rosetta Stone, some mummies, and a bunch of other old stuff.

CHAPTER 4
Bathroom Issues and Sensitive Parents

Tonight we headed to the theater to see *Les Misérables*; this is where my dad's sensitivity would be taken to a whole new level. Before I go into details, I would just like to take this time to explain the events taking place prior to this sudden outburst of sensitivity.

Well, as most of you may or may not know, *Les Misérables* is a pretty long show, and of course the first half is always the longest. One of the most painful feelings is when you have to go to the bathroom so badly that you are unable to walk, talk, or think about anything else. This is what I was experiencing the first half, but sitting in the middle of the row, there was no getting out, and of course when there was finally an intermission, there was a line of forty women for two toilets. I am sure many people have experienced a situation like this.

Anyway, as the play finished with a pretty much happy ending, and right before the lights are about to turn back on, I look over to my dad and see tears streaming down his face. When I say tears, I don't just mean one drop and he wipes his face, and that's it. I mean tears that kept running down his face onto his neck. When the lights came on I had the perfect opportunity to make fun of him for his sensitivity, and all he said was, "Hey, your dad's a sensitive guy; it's a good thing, and plus the ending was just so happy with him going to heaven and all." At that point all I could do was laugh and shake my head. To make matters even funnier, as I look around, there were only two other people crying, and they were old ladies.

When we headed to the train station, or the Tube as they call it in London, my dad and I had one of our "moments." These moments last about two to three minutes, when I get very annoyed with him, and he gets mad at me, and then something funny or entertaining distracts us, relieving the tension. This distraction happened tonight because we were having a moment. Because I was annoyed with him, he was trying to lighten the conversation, which distracted him from focusing on where or when our stop was approaching. Before we knew it, we were at the station past our stop and laughing while arguing about whose fault it was.

Jamie's Gems:

- Always use the restrooms before sitting down for a three-hour show.

- If you're annoyed with your dad, make sure it doesn't distract you or him from what's going on around you!

- Pick and choose your battles, because I can assure you there will be many.

CHAPTER 5

Paris—"When Daddy Met Sally"

Saturday morning began early; our adventure would continue to our next stop, Paris. To get to Paris, we had to go by train. By the time we arrived in Paris, we were both extremely hungry and ready for lunch.

Now here's another story. I don't know if any of you have heard of the movie *When Harry Met Sally*, but if you have seen it, you know the kind of person Sally is. Sally is an extremely picky eater and can never order anything straight from the menu. For example, in one scene of the movie Sally asks for pie. "But I'd like the pie heated, and I don't want the ice cream on top. I want it on the side, and I'd like strawberry instead of vanilla if you have it. If not, then no ice cream, just whipped cream but only if it's real. If it's out of the can, then nothing."

When we arrived at lunch the old woman next to me was eating some sort of pasta dish that looked like mac and cheese, but then she cracked an egg and mixed the yolk and ham into the pasta. That of course would not do, and so I just asked for the pasta plain. From then on, at every meal my dad has referred to me as Sally to everyone we meet. At that lunch my dad and I got into a stupid little fight, but that lasted all of five minutes. Usually hunger and heat are the cause of many of our fights. To top off the fight, when we got the check, it was the most expensive lunch we both had ever had; that did not help our mood either. After lunch we walked around Paris, just to get a feel for where we were.

That night we went to dinner, and that was where we met Mike and Melinda. It all started when my dad ordered a bottle of wine, and then the waiter poured me a glass as well. This took us both aback since we had never experienced a situation like this, since the drinking age where we lived was twenty-one. My dad quickly told the waiter, "No, no, no, just for me." We both laughed, and I said, "I can't believe he thought I looked old enough to drink!" Little did I know the drinking age in Paris is sixteen. Next to us a man kindly interrupted by saying, "You're only sixteen? I thought you were definitely in your twenties." I told him that I wasn't, and then his wife responded by saying, "Well, I'm a school teacher, so I figured you were seventeen or eighteen." We talked to Mike and Melinda for the rest of our meal. We shared food and told stories, and by the end of the night I felt like I had known them for years.

When we left the restaurant my dad wanted to go see the Arch de Triomphe because he thought it would look cool at night. He told me I would need a jacket because it would be chilly out. Of course I told him I wouldn't need it because it wasn't that cold, and I don't get cold easily. But of course I found myself freezing and getting weird stares from the people around us, who probably thought I was crazy for not wearing a jacket.

Jamie's Gems:

- Your parents aren't always right, but sometimes they are! Listen to them.

CHAPTER 6

Versailles on a Sunday in July—Are You Kidding Me?

Today was the day we were taking our trip to Versailles. Little did we know that we would be waiting in line for two and a half hours just to get in. It was scorching hot, and the line appeared to go on forever. By the time we finally got in, I was ready to leave. The rooms and chambers in Versailles were remarkable, and so was the sweat dripping down my face from this non-air-conditioned palace. When we finally left Versailles we made a stop at the Eiffel Tower.

One cannot fully grasp the beauty of the Eiffel Tower unless seeing it face to face in all its glory. Now at this point in our day we had been in the heat for 90 percent of it, and we had been walking a lot! Well, that walk didn't even compare to the walk we had to do next. Oh, and I forgot to mention, when my dad and I took the train back to the hotel, we didn't get through the ticket barrier because we were using the wrong tickets. Luckily a nice lady took me through with her, but my dad still had no way of getting through, so he had to jump over the barrier. From that point on he didn't let me forget it, and he claims I was leaving him behind. But anyway, back to our long trek.

Rick's Revelation:

- *When traveling in the heat of the summer, sometimes it makes sense to have an umbrella with you!*

- *It's important to stay fit; you never know when you have to hurdle a turnstile.*

CHAPTER 7

The Tour de France—So What, I'm Tired!

After the Eiffel Tower we tried to catch a taxi back to our hotel. For some reason no cabs would take us so we just kept walking. All of a sudden we heard a man speaking French over a loudspeaker and a bunch of loud cheers. Of course my dad wanted to follow the noise instead of continuing our search for a taxi. As we approached the noise and crowd we discovered that we had just walked into the last moments of the Tour de France. As a British rider won for the first time in one hundred years the crowd cheered wildly, but all I wanted to do was get back to the hotel. I was exhausted and did not care about how monumental of an experience this was. As we searched for a way back, we realized there was no way to get back to the hotel besides on foot. After six miles of walking we found ourselves across the street from the Westin Hotel. If it could have gotten any worse it did. The street was blocked off because of the race; it was still running even though it had already been won. This meant we had to walk an extra two blocks to get back. When we arrived at the hotel we had to get dressed for dinner. Though dinner was good, it was the event afterward that was the most memorable.

CHAPTER 8

How a New Yorker Hails a Cab in Paris

We wanted to call a taxi from the restaurant, but we knew they would charge us immediately after getting the phone call; this is how it works in Paris, and before you get in the taxi you might already owe twenty US dollars. Instead we searched for our own taxi. This was when my dad pulled the ultimate New Yorker move. He saw a taxi coming and a man waiting for it, and he stepped in front of the guy and took his taxi. As the taxi began to move, the French guy in the middle of the road stopped it. We pulled over, and they yelled at each other in French. I guess the guy was angry that we took the cab, and before we knew it the Vietnamese French cab driver was trying to kick us out to let the other guy in. We said we would leave, but the French man told us to stay in the car. You could tell the driver was pissed because when he dropped us at the hotel he yelled at us to get out.

Jamie's Gem:

- Don't ever let your dad pull a New Yorker move, especially in a foreign country; it won't end well.

CHAPTER 9

Dad Loses It at the Louvre!

Today we went to the Louvre. Here we saw many historic paintings and sculptures. This may have been the biggest museum I had ever been to. There were so many people; I found it hard to move. When walking around the Louvre we encountered one of the most famous pieces of art of all time, the Mona Lisa. Whenever I thought of the Mona Lisa I thought of a big portrait, or let's just say bigger than a thirty-by-twenty-inch portrait.

As hundreds of people gathered around the Mona Lisa, we all had the same objective: to get a picture we could bring home to our friends and family to show them that we had been within three feet of this famous portrait. With that goal in mind people were pushing and shoving to get a front spot to take the photo. My dad and I were lucky enough to get a front spot, with a perfect view of the painting.

Since the Mona Lisa brought forth a crowd, that meant it also brought forth a variety of people. Standing next to my five-foot-six-inch father was a tiny Asian lady, I'd say about five feet tall. Though she was tiny, boy was she feisty. This lady pushed and elbowed my dad four times as she tried to get the perfect picture. My dad quickly lost all of his patience; in fact, the museum security guards were watching and could not believe the lady kept shoving my father. They thought it was quite comical, but I can tell you my dad was not amused! I had to restrain him and talk him out of elbowing her back; it was crazy!

My first experience of the Louvre!

Jamie's Gem:

- Don't underestimate the strength of a tiny person when fighting for a picture of the Mona Lisa because a picture is worth a thousand shoves!

CHAPTER 10

Crepes, Creeps, and Portraits

After leaving the Louvre, we decided to go see a church up on a hill, and to have lunch and look around at the artwork. For lunch I can honestly say I had the best crepe I have ever had. After lunch we had a portrait done of me. As he drew me, people surrounded to watch and compare the portrait to me, to see if we looked the same. As I sat waiting for my portrait to be completed, I noticed that a young, chubby French boy was standing behind my father observing my portrait. He leaned in toward his sister and whispered, rather loudly, "The artist made that girl look a lot skinner than she really is; he made her look a lot better."

Though my dad was hoping I wouldn't hear what the boy had just said, sadly I had. After hearing what this boy had said, I thought that the portrait was not a direct comparison to how I truly looked.

Obviously my dad believed this portrait was next to that of the Mona Lisa, because right when we got back from the trip, I walked into my bedroom to find the portrait of myself hanging above my wall. Now the portrait rests above my bed, and it is pretty amazing! It is a constant reminder of Paris and a special day with my dad!

CHAPTER 11

So That's Why My Dad Posts to Facebook!

Since my dad knows people wherever we go, he of course found a friend he knew, David Red Nemitz, living in Paris with his wife Ninette, or should I say that the friend found Dad! Dad met David when he was in the audience at a speech my father gave in Florida a number of years back, and they became Facebook friends. My dad is always posting pictures and updating his status on Facebook, which at times can be annoying, especially when he tags my brother Alex or me without our permission!

When we got back to the hotel after our adventure to Versailles, my dad posted pictures from the Tour de France on Facebook just before we went out to dinner. When we got back from dinner that night, dad's friend David had sent him a message that he had seen the pictures from the race and that he was now living in Paris!

My dad would call this a "welcome-to-my-life moment." He says that all the time when he runs into people or has awesome and unusual experiences while he travels.

That afternoon we met David up at Montmartre for a drink after my portrait was finished. I asked him about his wife, and he told me that they had moved to France so that his wife could be close to her family, since she was being treated for breast cancer. I could relate to that since my stepmom Jackie had fought the battle of her life, fighting breast cancer, only to recently lose the battle after eight years. I asked David if I could meet his wife Ninette, and he gave her a call so that we could all meet up for dinner on the Champs Elysees. At dinner I learned that if you don't close the menu, the servers won't come over to the table. As I conversed with David and his wife, I fell in love with her accent. She also had some of the best style I had ever seen, and she rocked a beret. After dinner we said goodbye and headed back to the hotel. We were leaving in the morning for Florence.

Jamie's Gem:

- Most of the time dads can be annoying, so enjoy the days he isn't. They don't happen too often! Ha ha ha…kidding?

CHAPTER 12

The Power of TripAdvisor

If I haven't told you yet, my dad is a motivational speaker. Now you may be asking yourself, "Why does that matter? Who cares?" Well, this is relevant to my next story. As a motivational speaker, my dad of course has many sayings he chooses to live by; one of these sayings is, "I've spent more money in worse places!" This philosophy comes in when he buys or does something stupid, and then loses money from it.

Well, here's what happened. Since we were leaving for Florence we had to check out of our Paris hotel. This meant paying for the hotel room, the Wi-Fi used, and the drinks we had. In the middle of the night my dad is known for having snacks or drinks. At this hotel he had a Coke and a Sprite, thinking that they would be about five or six dollars apiece. Now when he went to check the bill, it said that the two sodas were eighteen Euros or twenty-two US dollars for two cans of soda. If that didn't make my dad ballistic enough, the hotel charged him an extra two dollars on the cans as a donation to the UNICEF Foundation.

With that my dad went crazy and told them to take off the donation because he had spent enough on the drinks already! If you asked him, he'd say that was probably in the top five for his saying, "I've spent money in worse places." However, that's not where the story ends.

My dad loves the website TripAdvisor.com, and he uses it often when he is planning for his trips. He picks his hotels and restaurants in large part based on the reviews of the customers and the feedback from the establishments themselves, but in this case it's probably best to let Dad reveal the rest of the story.

Rick's Revelation:

- *I was so frustrated I got a bill from this hotel in Paris that came highly recommended by this site. Having spoken internationally several times a year I always use TripAdvisor to research my hotels and restaurants. I felt twenty-two US dollars for two cans of soda was ludicrous, and I have stayed at this hotel chain before with only the best experience possible. Upon checkout the front-desk staff was very uncooperative and had charged a donation to UNICEF without my permission. I posted a review on TripAdvisor explaining my frustration with this particular hotel. Within three hours the manager of the hotel responded on TripAdvisor, and the hotel removed the miscellaneous charges.*

- *If you don't A. S. K. you won't G. E. T.*

Jamie's Gem:

- Kids, if you want to spare your parents a minor heart attack I suggest staying away from all the mini refrigerators in hotel rooms, especially ones out of the country.

CHAPTER 13

Dad and I Tackle a Cow in Florence

Well, moving on, we flew to Florence that morning and unpacked our bags at the Brunelleschi Hotel. As we explored some of Florence, of course my dad had another friend he knew there. This meant spending another hour having drinks and coffee with his friend, Maurizio Matucci. Dad had met Maurizio on his last trip to Florence; his company produces some of the best olive oil in the world.

On that trip, my dad and Jackie went into a local restaurant because they saw that it was very crowded, and my dad always says when a restaurant is crowded with locals it's a good sign! They sat them at a table next to another couple, but the menu was all in Italian. The couple overheard dad and Jackie discussing their dilemma, and the woman introduced herself and said that she was from Boston and her husband was from Italy, but had lived with her in Boston for two years. The husband, Maurizio, asked my dad if it was OK for him to order their meal. Dad quickly jumped at the chance, and he said it was an incredible meal, and of course my dad stayed in touch with Maurizio on Facebook! What else is new?

After sharing a quick drink we headed back to the hotel, where I smelled this funky aroma. I couldn't figure out where it was coming from, and my dad didn't smell anything, so we left it alone; this would come back to haunt us and play a major role, especially when it came to my dad, for the rest of our trip.

On our first night we went to Gargini, one of my dad's favorite restaurants in Florence, owned by his friend Ivan.

That night my dad and I shared the best and biggest steak I have ever had; it was as if we were tackling a whole cow together. It was huge! This steak was called Bistec Florentine; we don't have this steak in the United

States, and it comes from a white cow called a Chianina. This restaurant was so good that we decided to eat there again on the last night that we would be in Florence!

Since it was our first day in Florence we didn't sightsee much, but knowing my dad we would make that all up tomorrow.

Jamie's Gem:

- Whenever you are eating out of the country, live by the phrase "when in Rome." Eat what you want and explore, explore, explore. This is a once-in-a-lifetime opportunity so try new things, and never worry about your weight or being healthy!

- Make sure to be nice to everyone you meet and attempt to stay connected; you never know when you will visit again, and it's just fun being a citizen of the world!

CHAPTER 14

I Thought History Class Was Over!

The word "busy" does not even begin to describe the day that we had on July 25. Throughout this trip my dad kept saying, "Do you know how much history you are getting right now?" and "This trip is like two years of your world-art classes in three weeks!" Well, you could say this day came close to proving him correct. You see, my dad is a big history buff, and he has always said if he were not a doctor he would have been a history teacher.

Today we went to four museums, all completely different. First was the Academia, where we saw the *David*, one of the most famous statues ever made. My first thought when seeing the *David* was "Wow, this is a lot bigger than I was expecting." When I thought of the *David*, well, I don't know exactly what I thought it would be like, but I didn't expect it to be so large.

Anyway, after visiting the Academia, we made our way to the San Marco Museum. No offense to the monks, but this was my least favorite museum of the trip. The only positive thing I can say about the museum was that it was small. The museum was basically a church where monks lived and showed all of their empty rooms. Exciting, right? It's hard to believe that after these two museums, the day was not even half over. Next stop, The Pitti Palace.

This I will admit was pretty cool as we took a look into the royal chamber and artwork. Afterward, I convinced my dad to take a quick stop for a lunch break; this is where I learned my dad's "hidden identity."

We finished up our lunch, paid the bill, and were about to get up and leave when our waiter sat down next to us and in a soft tone said, "Excuse me, are you on TV?"

"I'm on the Internet, but no TV. Ha ha," my dad responded.

"You just look so familiar, sorry for my interruption," he said and walked away. As he walked away I laughed to my dad at the thought of someone mistaking him for being famous.

My dad told me that when he was younger, people used to mistake him and his cousin for Bruce Willis (when they were both younger and thinner). He told me an old lady at a grocery once chased Cousin Jack because she thought he was Bruce Willis. I made fun of him the rest of the day for thinking he looked like Bruce Willis.

But moving on, our last stop was the Uffizi Gallery. This was the time in the day when I had hit my breaking point. I was exhausted, and honestly I couldn't stand to look at one more piece of art. After walking for forty-five minutes my dad could tell I was ready to leave, and he was too. I found a sign that said, "Exit," so we followed it out. For the next fifteen minutes we were led on a wild goose chase and at times were stuck behind a massive tour group. My dad still claims I led us out wrong, but I promise that was the only exit sign around.

Jamie's Gem:

- Know your limit. If you are tired during the day, don't push yourself, and don't be afraid to say you need a break or are done for the day.

CHAPTER 15

The Funky Smell That Knocked Out Dad!

When we arrived back at the hotel and made our way back to the room, I smelled something funky again. It was the same smell from yesterday, but this time my dad smelled it too. The smell was absolutely horrible; it could almost make you choke, and it wasn't going away any time soon! I packed up my bags as my dad went to the lobby to get us another room. Knowing him he wouldn't be staying in this room another night, let alone a few more minutes. When he came back he told me we were changing rooms. I of course knew this already and had my bags ready to go. As he bent over to zip his final bag, we heard a "pop," and then my dad yelled a four-letter word. He had popped his back when he was bending down and was now in excruciating pain, which would be with him the rest of our trip. Finally he got the strength to stand up and face the pain. We moved rooms, had to shower quickly, and made our way to Il Latino, where the next adventure was waiting!

CHAPTER 16

Come On. Bruce Willis? No Way!

Il Latino is a restaurant where they sit you with random people. Sitting down at our table we waited to see who would be joining us. In walks a man in his late twenties wearing an LSU shirt, with a blonde pretty woman, also in her late twenties. As they sat down we all shook hands and introduced ourselves. Their names were Jennifer and Jude, and they were from Louisiana. The two had just gotten married and were in Florence on their honeymoon.

While the food continued to come endlessly, we continued to converse, and once again another couple were shocked when I had to refuse the wine being offered to me. They said they thought I was twenty or twenty-one. Well, we came to enjoy their company, and I asked them if they wanted to join us on Friday night for dinner. We were going back to Gargini since we enjoyed it so much. They agreed to join us, and they said they just had to cancel their other restaurant reservation.

Now here is where the interesting story begins. Ivan, the owner of Gargini, and his family had operated this restaurant for thirty-seven years. Ivan's brother lived in New York for a while and copyrighted the original name Garga. This meant that when he came back to Florence, Ivan and his family were forced to change the name to Gargini! Ivan's brother opened another restaurant in Florence using the original name Garga and pretended like his restaurant was the original.

This story is important because when Jennifer pulled out her paper with the reservation and asked us if we had heard of the restaurant, we had! They had made the reservation at Garga, the brother's restaurant, because on TripAdvisor it was rated the best place to go!

This was false advertising as Gargini was truly the place to go! We told Jennifer and Jude to cancel their reservation; they would be joining us for a fine dining experience. After dinner we walked them over to Gargini to meet Ivan and have a drink. We showed Ivan the paper, and he shook his head, knowing that his brother was capable of doing something like that.

While we sat and talked, Jennifer told my dad that he looked like someone famous; she then said, "Bruce Willis," and my dad and I immediately broke out in laughter and explained what had happened earlier that day. Her husband Jude said he thought he resembled John Goodman, but I don't think my dad took that as a compliment. Well, right now my hand is tired from writing so I will end this night by leaving you with some gems.

Our new friends Jennifer and Jude at Il Latino.

Jamie's Gem:

- Make friends, because it benefits you so that you are with other people besides your parent.

- Everything happens for a reason. Life works in mysterious ways, so don't question it. Just go with it! You won't regret it, I promise!

CHAPTER 17

Dad's Day! Medieval Towns and Wineries

Since yesterday was an eventful day, my dad promised that we wouldn't have to go to another museum today. Instead, we would be taking a side trip with a driver to see Sienna, San Gimignano, and Chianti. Our first stop was the old medieval town San Gimignano. It is really known for its high towers, but this is where I got my first Italian dress.

Next stop on our day trip was Chianti, and we went to tour two different wineries. Even though the drinking age in Florence was sixteen, I found myself repulsed by even the scent of wine, using water and soda to get the wine down. At the first winery we ate lunch and got to explore the land. That is where we met the most beautiful horse and sheep; in fact, the wine was named after this old horse.

I thought the day was much more relaxing than yesterday; it was more of a "dad's day," considering I'm not the biggest fan of wine, and it was nice to tour in a limo with a driver who really knew the area.

We also went to Sienna, which was interesting since I remember most of the sites in Sienna from seeing the movie *Twilight*. By the time we got back to the hotel, it was already close to dinnertime, and I was starved!

Dad and me in the Tuscan countryside.

CHAPTER 18

Dad and I Make a Great Team!

When we got back to the hotel we had to rush and get ready because my dad had made reservations at another restaurant he found on TripAdvisor and that is where our next adventure began!

To start off, my dad and I had reservations at some restaurant down the street very close to our hotel, or so we thought! Little did we know that it would take two wandering Jews and two stops at the front desk just to find a restaurant that was two minutes away from our hotel. Once we got there we had a table outside, with stools as chairs. Well, if you remember, my dad popped his back, and he wasn't holding up well, and these chairs definitely weren't happening. With that we made our way back to the hotel for the third time to find another restaurant to go to.

Finally we went to a restaurant called Giostra, another one that my dad had eaten at on a previous trip to Italy. Once again, the wandering Jews were off, and we aren't called the wandering Jews for nothing. We got lost, and it took us twenty minutes to find the restaurant. The worst part was that my dad had been to the restaurant before, and he still had no idea where we were going. Luckily when we arrived they had a table waiting for us.

As we ordered our meals, an older couple walked through the door. My dad had recognized these people from dinner last night, especially the woman. My dad claimed the woman was wearing the same dress from the night before when we saw her at Gargini.

Now let me say since my dad is from New York, he has that New York sense. This means that he can tell if someone is from New York, and he could tell this couple was for sure. The easiest description I could give of her is that she was a Joan Rivers lookalike, except extremely skinny. Behind us there was a young couple whom we would meet in a few minutes. As I sat eating my gnocchi, which was fair at best, I looked up and saw the Joan Rivers lookalike waiving at me. I looked around to see if she could have been waving at someone else, but I realized she really was waving at me.

I casually smiled and said to my dad, "That woman just waved at me; do we know her?" Before he could answer, the woman and the man were walking toward us. At first they stopped by the table behind us and engaged in a short conversation that I couldn't really hear, but before I knew it she was standing at our table.

My dad told her that he remembered seeing them last night at dinner, and then suddenly she was on a rant about her ex-husband, or not yet ex of four years, and how he had had taken her to that restaurant all the time, and that the man she was with was her boyfriend. From there the conversation only went downhill. What she asked next I couldn't even comprehend; she asked me if my dad was my husband!

I gave her a weird look and laughed, saying, "Noooo, he's my dad!"

She responded by saying, "Well, how would I know?" I really had no words for her at that point, so I just sat and let my dad do all the talking.

"Are you from New York?" he asked. She said yes and told us where she lived. She asked us where we were from, and I said St. Louis, while my dad said he was from New York, but lived in Florida. She must have been on something, because even though I said I was from St. Louis she asked me if I knew a girl named Alex who worked at a store in a New York mall. Not only did I not live in New York, but also my dad said she had named an old woman's department store that had gone out of business! At that time, I couldn't contain myself. I turned the other way, trying to cover my face with my hair, and I laughed. I tried to hold my laughter, but my dad could tell what was happening.

I was about to have a moment, the kind where I can't stop laughing! This lady would not leave the table, and when my dad told her he used to be a doctor, she lifted up her skirt and asked my dad if he knew what was wrong with her knee. She said she hurt it doing workouts in bed. He politely responded by saying he was not sure, but that she should get it looked at.

Luckily at that point the woman was done talking to us, but now the man was engaging us in conversation.

He told us he owned a chain of restaurants called Ciprianni. Now before I go on, I must tell a story. Ever since my dad was last in Europe, he has complained about this one meal he had at a restaurant. He had ordered a veal chop, but when he got it, it was so tough that he took one bite and then sent it back. The waiter told him he had eaten too much and had to pay for it. Since then he has not let go of the $230 meal! Well, back to the point. Standing in front of us was the owner of the restaurant that my dad had his awful experience at. As I said in the beginning, everyone is somehow connected, and here was another example.

When they returned back to the table, my dad and I laughed while trying to comprehend what had just happened. The man behind me turned around and also joked about the older couple.

His name was Joe Redi, and he turned out to be one of the largest leather manufacturers in Florence; he was with his girlfriend Hana, who had just opened her own designer-dress company called Peridot, and she was an up-and-coming fashion designer. As we engaged in intellectual and normal conversation with them, we decided to invite them to join us for dinner the next night at Gargini with Jennifer and Jude. Tomorrow would be a fun day, and I was excited to end it all with a dinner at my new favorite restaurant in Florence with our new friends! My dad was right; we truly were becoming citizens of the world!

Jamie's Gem:

- It's good to plan a relaxing day on a busy trip. Make sure you have at least one.

- Everyone is connected, and everything happens for a reason. Accept it!

- Meet people wherever you go; sometimes it will give you a good laugh and bring you closer together with your parents.

CHAPTER 19

Venice—The Hottest Place on Earth!

Today was another day for the wandering Jews; only today we were taking on a new location: Venice. To start off the day, my dad and I again got off at the wrong station. This meant an extra forty-five minutes of waiting for the train, and then riding the train to Venice. When we arrived in Venice, the first thing I noticed was the scenery. It was a sight you would see on a postcard. One of those pictures you would think someone would have to edit to make it look so beautiful, when really it's breathtaking on its own. I must say though, we could have left after seeing the view from the train station, because the rest of our trip to Venice was nothing that needed to be done again.

If someone would have told me it was 150 degrees out I would have believed him. Now my dad is known for sweating; whether we're sitting in a restaurant or lying by the pool, he is always sweating! Since my dad sweats in a restaurant when it's seventy-something degrees, imagine how much he was sweating in this hundred-degree weather! Let's just say it looked like he had taken three showers that day. Anyway, getting to Venice we had a destination in mind: St. Mark's Square.

Little did we know that it would take us an hour just to find this destination! Our excitement had immediately risen when we saw the sign and arrow pointing us toward where we wanted to go. That excitement soon faded as we went on a wild goose chase following these signs. These signs just kept appearing. I thought that the place we wanted to go to didn't exist.

Well, after an hour of wandering in zigzags, I was proven wrong. We had arrived at the subpar location we had been looking for. At that point, all we wanted to do was escape the heat.

We walked into a restaurant and sat down. As I was being "Sally," in my dad's words, I ordered buttered noodles. When the meal was finished we realized that just like our first lunch in Paris, we had been once again ripped off! Not only were we being charged for our meals, but also for air conditioning, sitting down, and getting bread, even though they bring it to you without even asking.

At that point my dad and I were both hot and upset, and we started our process of heading back. I had never been on a gondola ride, so as we walked back, my dad and I decided to take a quick ride on one. Though it was a very relaxing and fun experience, I couldn't get past the man singing the whole time. I guess in the job he's supposed to sing to the people in the boat, but I found it awkward and funny, one because he couldn't sing, and two because he was trying to be romantic.

Little did he know that he was singing to a father and his daughter. After getting off the gondola, we made our trek back to the train station, where we hoped to get an early train back.

We were three hours early for our original train, but we were ready to head back to Florence. When we got to the station they said that there were no more seats on the next train that was coming in forty-five minutes. They said that there were a few more first-class seats, but besides that, we would have to wait for our original train. At this time, my dad went back to one of his mottos, and as he paid for two first-class tickets he said, "I've spent more money in worse places," and then we sat and waited for the train. Of course having air conditioning in the first-class cabin was too much to ask for, because with our luck we ended up in the only cabin without air! For those next two hours, I watched as my dad was still sweating and could not get comfortable.

When we arrived back in Florence my dad and I were more than ready to relax in the hotel for a while before dinner with Jennifer, Jude, Joe, and Hana. Tonight was our last night, and we would be ending our trip here as we began, with dinner at Gargini. Only this time, we had brought friends we had met on our journey. Sitting at dinner we discussed our day in Venice, since Jennifer and Jude would be heading there tomorrow. We talked about staying in touch, and we all exchanged information. Joe would be coming to Florida at the beginning of the school year, and he would go to a football game with my dad.

It's amazing the people you will meet in life if you are just willing to put yourself out there. What I find to be even more amazing is that sometimes these people teach you more about yourself than you ever knew, and that even though you may have just met them, after two hours of dinner, it can feel like you have known them your whole life.

Dinner with our new friends at Gargini. Hana, Joe, Me, Dad, Ivan, Jude, and Jennifer

Jamie's Gem:

- Taking a side trip might seem like a good idea, but sometimes it doesn't always turn out great. When this happens, don't be afraid to change your itinerary; your trip doesn't have to be scheduled. Go with the flow!

- Realize that even though you may not enjoy what you are doing, or the heat you are experiencing, this moment or moments will turn into memories, so try to make light of the situation and don't complain too much. I guarantee if your dad or parent knew it would be like this, he wouldn't have taken the day trip, and it's not his fault.

- Everything comes together at the end of a trip. The friends you make, the fights you had, and the sights you had seen. Take everything in and try to start each new trip with a clean slate. In my case a clean slate would begin again in Rome.

CHAPTER 20

My First Visit to the Vatican—So That's What a Pope Looks Like!

Today was our last train, and we were headed to Rome. Right when we got to our hotel, our new guide, Agnes Crawford from Understanding Rome, was waiting for us, ready to take us to the Vatican, Sistine Chapel, and St. Peter's Basilica. The tour of the Vatican was very interesting, and I found myself able to tie together information I had learned during the school year to the sculptures and paintings I saw. Though the Sistine Chapel was packed, and the seventy guards were telling people to shhhh, I still thoroughly enjoyed looking at the extraordinary masterpieces.

I remembered learning in world civilization class about the Sistine Chapel and Michelangelo, so when I pointed out to our tour guide the person in the portrait who is said to be Michelangelo, she was thoroughly impressed. I found Saint Peter's Basilica to be magnificent and breathtaking, but I found seeing the popes' bodies inside to be a little eerie, but maybe that's because I'm Jewish. I guess that's why I just couldn't relate or feel the emotions others around me were feeling. When our tour was over, I was beyond ready to head back to the hotel before meeting up with one of my dad's speaker friends, Michael Domitrz, and his family to go on a tour of the Coliseum that night.

Agnes and me touring the Vatican.

CHAPTER 21
So What's the Problem!

Dinner with the Domitrz family was nice, though it was awkward at times since they had four boys, all of whom were a tad shy. Luckily toward the middle of our night with them, we all kind of warmed up to each other. Either that or it was our common view of the tour guide that brought us all together. I could safely say that this woman was probably the worst tour guide I have ever witnessed.

Whenever someone would ask a question she would say, "What's the problem?" and when the tour was over, all she said was, "OK, bye" and "Follow the black cat out." The problem with that was there were many wandering cats all throughout Rome and the Coliseum. Luckily for us one just happened to be leaving the Coliseum when we were about to exit. As we were leaving we all laughed and talked about how cool the Coliseum was and how awful the woman was as a tour guide. We made a quick stop for some gelato outside of some ruins and then said our goodbyes. Day one in Rome was over, and tomorrow would be our last day before heading to Israel.

Jamie's Gem:

- Be open to learning and seeing sites out of your comfort zone; you won't regret it.

- Sometimes it's not about the tour, but rather the company you are with that determines your take on the night. After all, the company, along with a bad tour guide, makes the best kind of story.

CHAPTER 22
The Difference Between a Cool Dad and a Chill Dad!

Earlier that day my dad and I had a debate on the difference between a "cool" and a "chill" dad. My dad thought he was cool, and I told him he isn't cool, but he is chill at times. I meant that in certain situations, he reacts in a calmer manner than most parents would.

CHAPTER 23

Ancient Rome—The Day I Met My Dad!

Today was day two in Rome, and our second day with our tour guide Agnes Crawford. This was a pretty relaxed day, which consisted of touring ancient Rome and the Forum. After sightseeing all we could by foot, my dad and I said goodbye to our tour guide and went to lunch.

At this lunch I realized that even though I have known my dad my whole life, there was still so much I didn't know about him. For example, on a lighter note, my dad went to the Olympic trials for hockey but was injured, and from then on he couldn't continue his ice hockey career. I also learned the story of how my dad and stepmom Jackie met. Some may call it a coincidence, but I call it fate.

One day my dad was on a boat with his friend Glen Berger, and he asked him if he knew anyone to set him up with. Glen gave him the number of a lady named Jackie Klein. My dad called her, but she never answered. That night on Christmas Eve he was going to the Matzo Ball (a Jewish singles party on Christmas Eve). He saw a woman leaving, and he walked up to her and told her she should smile. He asked her to dance and then asked her what her name was. She said her name was Jackie Klein. My dad immediately whipped out her number and said, "I'm Rick Goodman. My friend was setting us up!" After that, they stayed together, dad moved down to Florida and eventually got married.

Later on during lunch the conversation got a little deeper, and this was when I learned the reasoning behind my dad's constant "I love you" moments. My dad tells my brother and me everyday about twenty times that he loves us. Now it might sound awful, but it does get a little annoying. Well, during lunch I learned that as he grew up, his dad never once said I love you. The first time he ever said, "I love you" was when my dad was in his forties. Because of this my dad feels the need to tell us he loves us all the time so we don't forget it.

Well, as we finished our talk and paid the bill, we headed back to the hotel to relax before dinner.

Tonight would be our last night in Rome, and my Dad was excited to take me to his friend Paolo's restaurant, which was called Hosteria Antica Roma. Paolo's restaurant is located on the Appian Way, this famous Roman thoroughfare surrounded by ancient catacombs. The food was delicious; in fact, we had a lasagna recipe that was over a thousand years old. Paolo was great company and told many jokes and stories, but now it was time to go back to the hotel to finish packing for our next stop, Israel!

Jamie's Gem:

- Take the opportunity to be alone with your parents to get to know them better. This will help you to understand the reason behind some of your father or mother's actions or thoughts. This can only bring you closer.

- There is always something to learn, so learn it.

CHAPTER 24

Going Home—The Land of Israel

Flying to Israel was a moment I would never forget. There was something about the energy on the plane that made my heart beat faster than ever before. It is impossible to describe or recall all of the emotions I felt at the time our flight descended, but I can try to summarize simply by stating that I was home. Never had I felt so Jewish, and then when the Israeli music played when we landed, and everyone cheered, I had never been so proud and happy to be a Jew. I can't speak for my father, but when the music played, and I sang along and was a part of this celebration, butterflies coursed through my body as a sign of excitement, and I had never felt so united, so part of something in my entire life. This alone, the emotions, the songs, and the people…this was the memory that would last a lifetime.

The best part was having the chance to experience it with someone I love, and this moment would unite us even more. I knew this at that moment, and that is why I cherished the memory all the more.

After we grabbed our luggage from the Tel Aviv airport, we drove about an hour to Jerusalem. This was where we would be staying with Maggie (Mamacita, as I now call her) and Stewart Greenberg. Once again they were good friends of my dad's. Stewart and Maggie had gone on the mission to Israel with my dad and Jackie a few months back, and he was now living in Israel with Maggie for three months, going through a new cancer treatment at Hadassah Hospital.

When we arrived at the house I was in awe. Stewart and Maggie were so welcoming, and their house was magnificent, and for that moment I felt not like a tourist but like a true Israeli citizen. We were now living in Yemin Moshe, a community that overlooked the Old City. No longer were we cramped up in a hotel room; rather, we were living among Israeli people and neighbors to the Israeli people, and once again, I felt the unity.

As I unpacked my clothes, I met Maggie's son Anthony. He had been visiting them for the past three weeks, but he was leaving tomorrow. Since we got in around the afternoon, we relaxed a little and then headed out for dinner. Being "Sally," I ordered a hamburger for dinner, but it was surprisingly pretty good. We quickly finished dinner and were ready to explore what we could that night.

Maggie's son Anthony and me.

CHAPTER 25

The Western Wall (Kotel)

As we walked the streets of Jerusalem, we made our way to the Western Wall. This was also a moment and an image that will stick with me forever.

The Western Wall lit up at night was probably one of the most breathtaking sites I had ever seen. As Maggie and I headed down the girl's side, my father, Stewart, and Anthony went to the men's side. Now I have said many times that I am unable to describe or explain a moment that has affected me greatly, but I must now say it again. As my hand pressed against the wall, it was as if my mind flashed back in time to all of the people in my life who had had an impact on me. All of the people whom I loved and cared for who were sick, or just needed guidance, and those who just needed to be reminded of how they were loved and cared for.

At that moment I understood the meaning of prayer, I understood forgiveness, and I understood the importance of love. I was not alone. As I watched the other Jewish women around me engage in prayer, I felt comfortable doing the same. We stood and prayed, and when we finished praying we held hands and walked backward toward the entrance we had just came from. We met up with the boys in front of the wall, and we stood looking at the wall in silence for a few moments. I felt enlightened, and it was a great feeling. Though we all wanted to explore some more, we retreated to the house and went to bed. Tomorrow would be a busy day. Actually everyday would be, because there is so much to see in Israel. It is impossible to experience all of it in a short period of time.

Jamie's Gem:

- When you experience a life-changing event or moment with someone you love, let it unite you and bring you closer. Those are the moments you will remember, not the stupid fights you have.

- Allow yourself to be enlightened and allow yourself to step out of your comfort zone and be a part of something new.

- Enjoy every moment with the people you love and experience each life-changing journey with an open mind and a fresh start.

CHAPTER 26

Jerusalem—The Old City Tunnels and Tales

Today was our first official day in Israel. We went with our tour guide, George Horesh, to tour Jerusalem; included in our journey would be the City of David, the Western Wall Tunnels, the Church of the Holy Sepulcher, and finally Hezekiah's Tunnels. There are many times in my life when I wish I were taller, when I blame my mom and dad for being so short and in turn making me so short, but there are also times in my life when I enjoy being short and would hate to have the burden of being tall. This was one of those times.

Our first stop was the tour of the Western Wall Tunnels. George dropped us off at the entrance and told us he would meet us in the Old City after our tour was over. The underground tunnels were interesting, and the tour guide was informative, even showing us a model of how the temple was built. When we exited the tour, George was waiting for us as promised, and on we walked up the Via Dolorosa, where Jesus made his final walk through the old streets of Jerusalem.

Our next stop was the Church of the Holy Sepulcher, which was very crowded with people of all nationalities from around the world praying and observing all the ancient religious artifacts that this beautiful church possessed.

CHAPTER 27

Watch Your Head, George. Duck!

After lunch we headed to the City of David and Hezekiah's Tunnel; it was a good thing that we were doing this now, because the heat in the Middle East was intense, and hopefully this would give us a little relief!

When we entered the Tunnel, George offered to hold our wallets and any documents in a plastic bag so they would not get wet. For about an hour we walked through a dark, narrow tunnel that was probably about five feet high at the shortest point and six feet high at the highest point. When you enter the tunnel you walk down a flight of stairs, and then there is a sudden drop, and the next thing you know the cold water from the tunnel is suddenly waist high.

Of course this depends on how tall or short you are, and if there was ever a time to be short, this was it! As we walked I listened to my dad struggling behind us, and then I would hear a yell, and I would turn around to see that my dad wasn't paying attention and had hit his head.

This happened one time with our tour guide, George. He and I were both laughing as my dad struggled to keep up and take pictures at the same time. Suddenly, as I was laughing at Dad, George let out a yell that almost scared me! He banged his head so hard on the tunnel ceiling that we had to stop to take a little break before he could continue. Once again Dad and I had one of our moments! We laughed so hard that we were crying for a few minutes in the tunnel, with freezing cold water now up to our knees; it was a moment to remember.

Though we may have gotten some bumps and bruises along the way, I think the tunnel was my favorite part because we escaped the heat for a short period of time. Since the day had been very tiring, we relaxed and had a quick dinner with Maggie and Stewart in Jerusalem and enjoyed the sites.

George and me in the tunnels.

CHAPTER 28

A Birthday Surprise in Yemin Moshe!

My seventeenth birthday was tomorrow, so right around midnight my dad came in my room to sing, "Happy Birthday" to me with Maggie and Stewart. This is an old family tradition. We call each other over the phone and sing, "Happy Birthday," especially when we are in different cities. However, I am still trying to comprehend to this day the event that happened next. At exactly midnight the doorbell rang, and we all four raced around the house trying to figure out who it could be. The whole time I thought the three of them knew who it was and that they were messing with me, but they weren't.

We all approached the door and ran through the possibilities. Maybe it was Anthony coming back, maybe Alex (my brother), or Jackie? Or maybe it was a package from my mom? As we opened the door we were all proven wrong. My dad and Stewart looked through the peephole and noticed two people standing at the door: a man and a woman, and the woman had a gift!

Stewart opened the door, and they introduced themselves to us, and that is when we met Yaachov Sonnenschein and Shayna Letter, our neighbors. Apparently they had been walking back from a wine tasting at the Israeli Museum, and Yaachov tried calling his friend to wish him a happy birthday. When they heard us singing he hung up the phone and stopped by to sing, "Happy Birthday" to me! In they walked, bearing a gift: a bottle of Israeli olive oil. As we sat and talked for about an hour, we all kept discussing how crazy this whole situation was. Before they left, we all exchanged information, hoping to meet up sometime before we left. As I lay in bed, I couldn't help but think, "Wow, it's funny how life works."

Jamie's Gem:

- Sometimes you just need to sit back and watch life take its course. Life is a weird concept to try and figure out, so don't try. Sit back and remind yourself that everything happens for a reason.

CHAPTER 29

My Seventeenth Birthday—A Step Back in Time

The heat of summer in the United States is nothing compared to the heat in the desert of Israel. It's deadly. Waking up from our crazy night, I ran into the kitchen to see the olive oil. I wanted to make sure that I hadn't just dreamt about my incredible birthday surprise. After realizing I was not making things up, I headed to Masada with my dad and George.

The time on Masada was not just memorable because of the extreme heat and the history of the site, but also because of the hat my dad was wearing. He bought the most ridiculous and most embarrassing hat I have ever witnessed!

Not only did he buy it, but also he wore it in public! If we were anywhere but Israel I would have pulled the "I don't know you" card, but I figured, what the heck, and I just made fun of him for the duration of the trip.

The highlight of today was heading to the Dead Sea, and I never could understand how a person could just float without sinking. Well, as we made our way down to the water my dad and I decided to "go big or go home." By that I mean we covered our bodies head to toe in mud, and then went into the sea. I have to say that this moment was one of the best experiences of my life, and I think it brought my dad and me a lot closer together.

Today we laughed and joked and didn't fight or get annoyed with each other. It was as perfect as a day could have been, and I only wish that I had realized that then.

For the first time in the whole trip, I think my dad was "Sally." At lunch we were only given a few options, so I went with the classic turkey on bread, and my dad found nothing he wanted so he settled for a candy bar. After finally leaving the Dead Sea, we headed off to our final stop: the Holocaust Museum Yad Vashem.

This was one of the most moving experiences of my life. Reading and watching the stories of the Holocaust victims and survivors will always bring me chills.

The Holocaust is the only thing in my life able to bring about a mixture of emotions. I cry and feel sorrow for those who died, I feel anger toward the ones who participated and watched, and then I feel happy and proud to read about all those Jews and non-Jews who helped and risked their lives for the sake of others, and in my heart that brings me joy.

Joy knowing that even in this horrific time there were still good people in the world, and maybe there was good in everyone, just deep down in some. But finally I felt proud, proud to call myself a Jew, and no one would ever take that away from me. The rest of my night was great. We went out to dinner for my birthday, and at the end of my night I could say, "Best birthday ever. Thanks, Dad!"

Jamie's Gem:

- Embrace the moments in life you can't ever get back, and hopefully you will realize how great they are at the moment.

- Allow yourself to form a closer relationship with your parents; they can be cool, some of the time…ha ha.

CHAPTER 30

Caesarea—Ancient Ruins Meet Modern Trash

Today was our last day with George, and we were going snorkeling in the Mediterranean. I'm usually not a fan of the ocean, but this was one of the most beautiful sites to see. Underwater we found ancient boats and anchors, but it was sad to see all of the waste people put into the ocean. At points I was swimming only through trash, and I couldn't believe people would want to trash such a beautiful creation. We explored three different time periods all under the water. I really think that people need to make an effort to clean up some of the trash to make this site even more beautiful! Hopefully, soon!

Of course a trip would not have been complete without going to a famous winery, so our next stop was a wine tasting at Tishbi Winery.

As my dad sat and tasted wine, I snacked on the free chocolates while trying to set up the wine-tasting girl (she was twenty-one) with my brother. We exchanged Facebook info and took a few pictures to send back to my brother, so who knows? Maybe he will end up with an Israeli girl.

I think the days were catching up to us because after the winery we were more than ready to return back to Yemin Moshe and take a nap before dinner.

Tonight we are heading out to an Asian restaurant, hoping to have a meal that isn't kosher. Surprisingly the food was amazing, and we all left feeling pretty satisfied. Before heading back we stopped next door to pick up a few groceries. Looking in the ice cream section, Maggie and I couldn't believe that we found Ben and Jerry's Chubby Hubby ice cream. Sadly they stopped making it in the United States, but today we were able to have it in Israel!

CHAPTER 31

Shopping and Shot Glasses

Today was the day I felt like a true Israeli. For the first time throughout our whole trip we were not acting like tourists, but rather as natives of the land. Since it was Friday (the Sabbath), Maggie and Stewart took my dad and me to the Shook Market. This was probably one of the most chaotic places I have ever been to, and I enjoyed every minute of it. The Shook was basically an open market with anything you could probably ask for, right in front of you. From fish to candy and clothes, spices, and fresh baked goods we saw it all.

Maggie, Stewart, and me at the Shook.

Of course the market was packed because everyone was in a rush to buy food for the Sabbath that night. As we bought our food and challah, my dad and I explored and shopped while Maggie and Stewart returned home. Walking the streets of Tel Aviv we visited dozens of stores that were both for my dad and me on Ben Yehuda Street. Just like any other day on our trip, something interesting, good or bad, was bound to come between Dad and me.

Dad and me heading to Ben Yehuda street.

This is how it all started. Back at home before our trip, I asked my friends if they wanted me to bring back any souvenirs for them. My friend Annalise collects dozens of shot glasses, and so she requested I bring her back one. The other girls had no idea what they wanted, but they all had a few shot glasses so they asked for one as well. Of course I had saved getting the souvenirs for the very last minute, and so here we were in Israel with the trip almost over.

SHOPPING AND SHOT GLASSES

My dad reacted how many parents would have reacted; my dad was confused at why kids would want a shot glass and told me I had to use my own money, which I was going to do! So I bought the glasses, and we walked around. I was getting annoyed at my dad because he kept making me try on clothes that I didn't like, clothes that he thought were "cute." Every time I told him he didn't have good style (for my clothes type), he would get offended and go on a rant about his ex-girlfriends and my mom and Jackie, and he talked about how he had bought them all their clothes. Anyway, once again he was making me try on these ugly clothes, and I'll admit, I had an attitude, but all of a sudden I heard a bag drop.

Right then I knew it was the bag of shot glasses. We pulled them out, and one was broken. Of course I got a little annoyed, but right away my dad's mood changed, and he went on a rant, storming out of the store and saying it's my fault and how teenage girls shouldn't have shot glasses (true but beside the point). Being the dad he is, he of course expected an apology, which my stubborn self was not willing to give.

As we walked home I strayed ahead of him, and when his mood changed back to normal and happy, mine remained annoyed, and I wanted to go back to the house. When we returned home we had a few hours to rest before it was Shabbat, and we would be visiting the Western Wall.

Rick's Revelation:

- *For all the fathers who want to choose clothes for their teenage daughters, I say leave it up to mom or your daughter; it is significantly less stressful!*

CHAPTER 32

Shabbat at the Western Wall

The Western Wall at night was magnificent, but the wall at night on Shabbat was even better. Hundreds of people gathered by the wall, and as the men separated from the women, you could tell which men belonged to which so-called sect. The women were singing and dancing, along with youth groups who were my age. Among all the people, what impressed me the most was all of the soldiers who were dancing and singing with their rifles over their shoulders, and at that moment I felt as one with all of the people.

Though we were all strangers, I felt as though I knew them personally, and we all shared these two important features: our love for Israel, and our love and pride for being Jewish. It's at these moments in your life when you can't believe that hate in our world even exists. Seeing the pride and happiness within this community makes me question what the world would be like if we all lived this way. In a sense this question seems impossible and unrealistic, but in an even greater way it makes me question, "Why? Why does most of the world hate to see one another thrive, and are we all selfish enough to put the needs of ourselves before the unity of a nation?" Walking home from the wall I asked these questions to myself. When we returned home we cooked dinner, said our prayers, and ate. I can't remember the last time before that night that I sat down for a Sabbath dinner, but that night I realized all I had been missing and wished I could have had these dinners more often. I went to bed that night not thinking of the silly arguments with my dad or really anything about our relationship, but rather I thought of the Western Wall. I thought about all those prayers people stick into the wall, and I wondered if any of these prayers were answered. This was the moment I felt the closest to God, to my religion, to Israel, and to myself.

Maggie, Stewart and me at the Kotel

CHAPTER 33

The Best Decision I Ever Made!

When my dad expressed his interest in spending three weeks traveling Europe with me, I was filled with excitement, yet I was also hesitant. I must admit that I have always been a momma's girl, and my relationship with my dad was a confusing one. Though I had always fantasized about having this close bond with my dad, one in which I would feel comfortable telling him anything, and asking him for advice, I could never get myself to feel this bond. Embarking on this trip would mean living alone with my father for over three weeks, and not being able to escape him or run to my room when he annoyed me. Though I acknowledged that my dad and I may butt heads, I also realized that this would be a once-in-a-lifetime opportunity, and I would be stupid to pass it up.

I cannot express how thankful I am now that I did not turn down this experience. The places I saw, the history I learned, and the bond I created with my dad is one that will be solidified in my mind for the rest of my life. Traveling with my dad forced us to confront our issues with one another and allowed us to work out our problems rather than run away from them or keep them buried inside.

After our journey together we came out as different people; I knew more about my father, and he knew more about me. Though this journey brought us closer together, sadly, what solidified our new relationship was the passing of my stepmom Jackie. Before she passed I would call my dad each day to see how he was doing, and once she passed we spoke many times a day. Before our trip to Europe and before Jackie became extremely ill our phone conversations consisted of, "How was your day?" and then I would say, "Good" or "The same as every other day," something sassy like that. Our conversations seemed forced and boring, but after our trip and Jackie, we speak all the time. We engage in heartfelt and lively conversations, and for once I actually look forward to calling him and hearing his voice each day. I have never been a very lovey-dovey person like my dad, but after Europe and the passing of my stepmom, I always say the phrase my dad tells me almost every day after our phone calls: "I love you more than the universe."

This trip taught me a lot about my father and myself, and it allowed me to experience other cultures. I am so happy and thankful I traveled to Europe, and I couldn't have asked for a better travel partner. I love you, Dad, and thank you for everything.

Our last night Dad and me outside the walls of Jerusalem.

CHAPTER 34

That's Not the End of the Story!

November 11, 2013

On our last day in Israel, my dad and I went to visit the Western Wall one last time. When we arrived I saw a large group of kids my age standing in a circle singing and dancing. Now don't get me wrong, I loved being on this trip with my dad, but I couldn't imagine how amazing it would be if I was in Israel with kids my own age. My father went up to one of the kids to ask them what trip they were on and they said they were attending Alexander Muss High School in Israel (AMHSI).

My father and I knew exactly what that was because my stepmom, Jackie, attended AMHSI when she was my age and talked about her experience all the time. When we got back from our trip, I thought about AMHSI a lot and my dad kept asking me if I wanted to go that following summer.

What I didn't tell you was that my dad and I originally took our trip together to escape our hectic life at home. We had become more distant, because he was upset all the time, because my stepmom was battling breast cancer for eight years. She had been a fighter, but it was clear our time with her was short. Both Jackie and my dad realized that his frustration regarding the cancer was taking a toll on our relationship, and so they agreed that we needed to get away for a while.

The trip went great, as you can see, but as I said before, I was hesitant about spending six weeks away from my family to go live in Israel. In fact I was hesitant for a few months after the trip, but my decision became clear in early February. On January 28th, 2013, Jackie passed away and I was devastated.

People always told me that even though someone may die, they will always be with you and watching over you. Well, I waited for the sign, a sign to show me that Jackie was with me, but I never felt it. That is when I decided to go back to Israel.

Israel was my final chance to search for Jackie. I believed that traveling to Israel and attending the same program that she attended, would allow me to feel a connection with Jackie. That is why I did AMHSI; not to explore Israel and learn about Jewish History, but to learn more about myself, and to look for a sign that Jackie was still with me.

I cannot express how much AMHSI and the Jewish National Fund (JNF) have impacted my life. As cliché as it may sound; Israel gave me a fresh start in life and my realization of that came on one of our Tiyuls. On this Tiyul we awoke at 3:30 am to begin our hike up Masada. The sky was pitch black, and the only light that could be found came from our teacher, Yossi's flash light. I will admit that I tend to stay away from anything involving fitness, but mysteriously for the whole hike up I was filled with energy.

My friends Sam, from Minnesota, hiked in front of me, while my friend Lauren, from Maryland, walked behind me. Throughout the entire hike we sang songs, made up our own raps about Masada, and the best part was that no one complained. I'm not sure if that's because we weren't tired or hot, or if it's because we all knew how amazing this opportunity was. As we reached the top of Masada I reached to grab my phone and I immediately called my dad and mom. "Dad, you will never believe where I am right now! I just hiked Masada and we are about to watch the sunrise!" Dad told me how incredible that was and how proud he felt.. As Dad hung up the phone he said, "Jackie would be proud."

As my group walked into the remains of the synagogue, we faced out to Jerusalem and prayed. With our arms around one another we cried of happiness and disbelief. We wept, because we were happy with what we had accomplished, and because we were moved by the story of Masada, and the strength of the Jewish people. After prayer, we toured around Masada, and then Yossi had us reenact the role of the Israeli soldiers. He would yell commands and in a matter of seconds we would be on the ground, crawling with only the strength of our arms.

Afterwards, we walked out to the edge of Masada and Yossi told us how Israeli soldiers must travel three days in the desert, and their last task is to hike Masada. Once they are on top of Masada, they stand where we were standing, and yell as loud as they can, the words, "AM YISRAEL CHAI, Masada shall not fall again!" We repeated it three times, "AM YISRAEL CHAI, Masada shall not fall again!"

That moment will be solidified in my memory for the rest of my life. I have never experienced something so empowering as I did screaming those words off Masada, and hearing our voices echo over and over again. It was at that moment when I finally felt the presence I had been looking for; Jackie's presence.

I could envision her standing there, just as I was, yelling those words at Masada; that same empowerment igniting her being... Jackie and I had hiked Masada, we had learned its history, we had reenacted the role of Israeli soldiers, and we had screamed "Am Yisrael Chai." Though our experiences were 35 years apart, it felt as if we were doing it together.

It was much hotter hiking down Masada, but the energy and inspiration I had been feeling carried me through the rest of the day, and the rest of the trip. To conclude our Tiyul we traveled to the Dead Sea. This is where we covered ourselves in mud, and carefully entered the salty water. Now, I loved every minute of Israel, but I must say that the Dead Sea is probably something I would do once, just to say I did it. The Dead Sea is the one place you get punished for being a good shaver. If I tell you the pain you feel in that sea if you enter with cleanly shaven legs, oh my, just no. Don't ever!

That was a very memorable Tiyul; however, every day in Israel was a memorable one. I made friends that I will keep for a lifetime, I learned independence, I learned Jewish history, and most importantly, I learned about myself. This experience made me proud to be Jewish. I was proud of my religion, and the person I had become.

Before this trip I admit that I questioned the existence of G-d. For the past eight years I had been watching one of the greatest people I know fight against cancer and it just didn't seem fair. But, I believe that everything happens for a reason. If it wasn't for Jackie and her passing when she did, I probably wouldn't be writing about my experience in Israel today. I am a new person, because of this program I have my dad, AMHSI and the Jewish National Fund (JNF) to thank for that.

Jamie Goodman

TRAVEL RESOURCES

Websites

Tripadvisor.com

AA.com

Kayak.com

Tour Guides and Drivers

Rome: Agnes Crawford

Web: www.understandingrome.com

Email: Info@understandingrome.com

Rome: Luke The Limo Driver

Web: www.lukethedriver.com

Email: Info@lukethedriver.com

Phone: 39 328 666 7898

Florence and Tuscany

Wine Tour in Tuscany: Donatella

Web: www.winetourintuscany.com

Email: Info@winetourIntuscany.com

Sorrento-Amalfi Coast

Francesco Marrapese

Web: www.francescomarrapese.com

Email: Info@francescomarrapese.com

Phone: 39 338 338 7393

Israel: Tour Guide and Driver

George Horesh

Email: George@Isradventure.com

Phone: 054 436 6970

JAMIE'S JOURNEY: "TRAVELS WITH MY DAD"

Hotels

Hilton London Tower Bridge

Address: 5 More London - Tooley Street, London SE1
2BY, England (London Bridge)

Web: www.hilton.com

Phone: 44 203 002 4300

The Westin Paris – Vendôme

Address: 3 rue de Castiglione 75001 Paris, France

Phone: 1 800 937 8461

Web: www.westin.com

Hotel Brunelleschi

Address: Piazza Santa Elisabetta 3 Via De Calzaioli, 50122 Florence, Italy

Phone: 39 05527370

Web: www.hotelbrunelleschi.it

Rome Marriott Grand Hotel Flora

Address: Via Vittorio Veneto 191, 00187 Rome, Italy

Phone: 1-866-576-5456

Web: www.marriott.com

Restaurants

Las Sourdiere

Address: 4 rue de la Sourdiere, 75001 Paris, France

Phone: 01 42 60 12 87

Web: www.lasourdiere.com

Trattoria Gargani

Address: Via del Moro, 48/r, 50123 Florence, Italy

Phone: 39 055 2398898

TRAVEL RESOURCES

Web: www.garganitrattoria.com

Note: Ask for Ivan

Da Il Lantini

Address: Via Palchetti 6/r, 50123 Florence, Italy

Phone: 39 055 210916

Website: www.illatini.com

Note: Ask for Mauriccio Mattucci

La Giostra

Address: Borgo Pinti, 10/12/18 R | 10/R 18/R, 50121 Florence, Italy

Phone: 055 241341

Web: www.ristorantelagiostra.com

Hostaria Antica Roma

Address: via Appia Antica 87, 00179 Rome, Italy

Phone: 065132888

Web: www.anticaroma.it/eng/index.html

Note: Ask for Paolo

Machnyhuda

Address: 10 Beit Ya'akov St., Jerusalem 94323, Israel (Givat Ram)

Phone: 972(0)25333442

Web: www.machneyuda.co.il

Eucalyptus

Address: 14 Hativat Yerushalayim, Jerusalem, Israel

Phone: 972 2 6253 090

Web: www.the-eucalyptus.com

Herzl
Address: Mamilla Ave. 13 | Mamilla, Jerusalem, Israel
Phone: 02-5020555
Web: http://www.herzl-mamila.com/

Travel Guides
Eyewitness Travel: Top 10 Florence and Tuscany
Rick Steve's Florence and Tuscany
Frommer's Italy

Educational Institutions
Alexander Muss High School in Israel
Address: 9 Aliyat HaNoar Street, Hod Hasharon, Israel 45102
Phone: 011 972 9 740 5705
Web: http://www.amhsi.org/

The Jewish National Fund
42 East 69th Street
New York, NY 10021
Phone: (888) JNF-0099
Web: http://www.jnf.org

ABOUT THE AUTHOR

Jamie Goodman is a senior at John Burroughs School in St. Louis Missouri and a graduate of the Alexander Muss High School in Israel. Jamie spends most of her time giving to others. She is the President of the ALS Club at John Burroughs School and is also a teacher's assistant in the Aim High Program working with children from low-income families to enrich their learning experiences.

In addition Jamie regularly volunteers her time at the Kuto Club working to prevent teen suicide and is an Official Buddy at the Special Olympics. Jamie is the Sports Editor for the John Burroughs School Newspaper and plans to pursue a Journalism degree after she graduates.

INDEX

INDEX

INDEX

Made in the USA
Monee, IL
13 July 2021